How to Pick Winning Stocks!

Jason Jenkins

Disclaimer

Before investing, consider the investment's objectives, risks, charges, and expenses.

Investors should be aware that trading stocks involves substantial risk of loss and is not suitable for all investors. There are no guarantees of profit no matter who is managing your money. Past performance is not necessarily indicative of future results. As with all your investments, you must make your own determination whether an investment is appropriate for you. The author is not recommending or endorsing any security. You should conduct research and perform a thorough investigation as to the characteristics of any securities you intend to purchase. Before investing, you should read the prospectus, offering circular, indenture, or similar document carefully for a full description of the product, including its features and risks, to determine whether it is an appropriate investment for your investment objectives, risk tolerance, financial situation and other individual factors, and be sure to re-evaluate those factors on a periodic basis. The information contained herein is provided for educational purposes only. Other information and / or advice may be more appropriate for your investment approach.

Table of Contents

Why This Book? 5

    Why Should You Care? 5

    What's Different about This Book? 6

    Are You Ready to Become Wealthy? 6

    Your Dividend Opportunities 6

    Picking Winning Stocks............................9

    Other Guidelines to Consider 10

    When to Sell 11

Putting It All Together.....................................14

You Have a Choice 16

A Final Note 17

Appendix - A Practical Formula 18

Investment Notes 21

Why This Book?

Wealth and Happiness – why not have them both?
In this book, you will learn how to build your wealth through dividend-paying stocks
This book will give you the motivation and the know-how to extricate your family from crushing debt and prepare for a comfortable retirement.
You can become debt-free, build up a reserve of emergency cash, and make sure that you never run out of money in your retirement.

Why Should You Care?

A Dividend-Paying Company is Less Risky than a Non-Dividend-Paying Company

A dividend-paying company has always been less risky than a non-dividend-paying company. A dividend paying company pays dividends with cash, which can not be easily manipulated like the company's stated earnings. Dividends, therefore, are a more stable part of total returns. In addition, dividends are always positive.

Paying a dividend imposes a certain manner of discipline on the company's management, and makes them more sensitive to the potential cash flow impacts of new projects and new approaches.

By implementing a culture of dividend payment, company management is less likely to indulge in "empire building", and also less likely to simply hoard cash, or rush headlong into mindless expansionism. Few U.S. companies that pay dividends are willing to cut dividend payments – to do so signals that the company is financially weak.

Your investment strategy in embracing dividend paying companies is the only way to accumulate wealth.

Reinvesting those dividends is the surest way to grow that wealth through the magic of compounding.

What's Different about This Book?

This book cuts through the dross. Instead of spending most of its pages telling you how great an investor, or how much stock knowledge I've amassed, you're going to see the exact process by which you can pick winning dividend stocks. You'll have the exact and laser-sharp knowledge where to look, what to find, and how to proceed.

Are You Ready to Become Wealthy?

Go ahead. Look at other books. Make your own assessment. Then, when you're ready, come back here. We'll "do this thing" together.

You won't be disappointed.

Your Dividend Opportunities

To paraphrase an old saying:

"Stock opportunities are like streetcars. One comes along every fifteen minutes!"

Of the myriad companies that offer dividends, only a few will be able to meet your exacting standards.

What are those exacting standards and what will you use to evaluate stock candidates?

There are only four yardsticks you have to use:

> a. Dividend yield
> b. Dividend growth.
> c. Dividend payout.
> d. Company P/E ratio.

Let's explore these yardsticks.

What's the "minimum" Dividend yield you should consider?

That's an easy one. You want to do better than the average investor, so that means you need to make more than what you'd get if you only invested in the S&P500 bundle of stocks. Currently (this is being written in 2020) that means your dividends need to bring in an annual return better than 1.8%. Let's double that number: your stock's dividend should be at least 3.6%

But wait! That's not the only element. You also need to consider inflation. In 2020, the forward estimate for inflation is 2.5%. Your stocks should make at least 2X that number. So the minimum stocks dividend you should consider is: 3.6% + (2.5% X2) or **8.6%**.

Let's round that up to **9%**.

Your guideline is clear: any stock paying out dividends equal to or greater than 9% is a definite candidate for your wealth portfolio.

What about "Dividend growth"?

Using the same criteria, let's set annual dividend growth at 2X inflation, or 5%, or better. That was easy. Personally, I try to select companies that have demonstrated a yearly dividend growth track record around 10%. A company's dividend growth needs to be looked at over the past 10 years. Has the dividend growth been consistent? Dump inconsistent payout companies.

Is that "Dividend payout" sustainable?

I recommend only considering companies whose dividend payout ratio is 35% -75% of current income. But that can be misleading: the company may be experiencing a temporary downturn, but has sufficient cash on hand and a sustainable cash flow to maintain paying dividends, even revenues have fallen for some reason. Here' you'll need to do some research.

Why consider the "Company P/E ratio"

The P/E ratio is a measure of what people think the stock is worth. A high P/E ratio means that the investor thinks the stock's worth far more than what the company's currently earning. This is usually an indication that the investors are willing to put up with current income levels that aren't that great, but are banking on the company catching fire in the future and really reaping in money. Most of the times that's optimistic and a sure path to failure.

I like to err on the conservative side. I find that companies that have P/E values at or below 20 are sound investments.

We discussed one of the tools available through your brokerage house: the "Stock Screener". This is an invaluable tool to help you sort through stocks.

When you invest in a dividend stock, you want to know if it will sustain its payouts and indeed, grow its payouts over time.

Your brokerage house's "stock snapshot" can tell you a lot of information: what the stock's dividends have done in the past (have they grown, fallen, remained constant?) It can tell you the current projected annual yield.

Validate the stated dividend yield by looking at each stock's snapshot page.

Toss out any candidates that have slashed their dividends recently.

Toss out any stocks that reveal that they really don't pay dividends.

Picking Winning Stocks

Use the brokerage house's "Stock Screener" tool and set the Stock Screener's basic search criteria:

a. Stock dividends equal to or greater than 9%

b. Stock dividends that have annual growth equal to or greater than 2X inflation.

c. Stock dividend payout ratios that are less than 75%.

d. Stocks that have P/E values below 21%

These criteria will give you the stock candidates that are most suitable for building your wealth.

I use another criteria, that of **affordability**. While you may be above those petty concerns, I find it a little painful to buy a stock that has a price too much above $25 a share. But that's just me.

I'll admit, I do have some rather expensive stocks in my portfolio. Some are over $100 a share.

And I do have some stocks that have dividend yields below 9%, too.

Its all a matter of discretion.

Other Guidelines to Consider

I repeat: Select only those stocks that have a price to earnings ratio less than 20 to 1. That will usually eliminate those companies that might be just a tad too risky, that are overvalued, and could collapse.

How about stock prices?

You might set a cutoff for stock prices that are comfortable for you.

Or just for a change, you might want to try some "high fliers" that have exorbitant dividend returns.

Don't plan on being a "Buy Them and Hold Them Forever" investor.

Your portfolio will change over time. You just might want to take a risk here and there. And you could just sell that stock next quarter if you feel it's too risky.

Don't buy any stock that has slashed their dividends more than 40% from last quarter.

They're probably in trouble, and are going to fail. But if the yield meets your criteria, you just might want to take a flier on them, too.

When to Sell

Every stock purchase you make should be made as if you were going to hold that stock forever. Remember, every time you buy or sell a stock, your stock broker gets paid. Your broker doesn't care what your goals are, or what stocks you purchase, as long as you do your trading through him/her. That's a recipe for potential disaster.

So, buy your stock as if you're going to hold on to it forever (and incidentally, force your broker to wait a very long time for a sales commission!).

But there are situations that will require you to re-evaluate your position.

Those situations are (in no particular order of importance):

a. **A stock cuts its dividends.** This is a big red flag: The company has just publicly declared that it has some serious financial problems. Get out now. Later, if the situation reverses, you can always buy back in, but during the crisis period, you're safely away.

b. **The company is acquired by another.** Another red flag: either the company is so cash rich that it's an easy takeover target, or the company is a lamb that's been acquired so it can be sheared of all of its cash. Beware! This may be a situation that bears further investigation.

c. **The company grows too fast** and its price to earnings ratio begins to get out of hand. That could signal a dividend cut if the company fails to live up to its expectations. Again, a heavy watch is necessary. I caution all that P/E ratios above 20 may signal a too-risky investment. Look elsewhere!

Plan to re-visit all of your stock portfolio companies at least once a year, perhaps twice a year and make sure that the reasons why you bought that stock are still germane.

Incidentally, if you have a stock that has paid out dividends for a long period then simply freezes its dividends, that freeze may not be a cause for alarm. It may merely signal that the management is re-evaluating its position and is taking a breather. Don't sell unnecessarily.

However, if the dividend falls or is eliminated after a freeze, dump it like a bad habit: the company is in serious financial trouble.

You are also making money by buying stocks that grow their dividends. If a stock cuts or eliminates dividend growth, it just may be time to ditch that stock and look at some other stock that has a more positive outlook.

But one indicator that really isn't an indicator, per se: the payout ratio. If you have a stock that had a healthy payout ratio (below 75%) and the payout ratio jumps, look closely at that stock's other indicators to see if that payout is sustainable. If the company has ample cash on hand, and is experiencing a minor crisis or setback, it could ride out that anomaly without materially disturbing its dividends. After all, dividend payments are sacred.

I'll repeat: for a company to cut its dividend payments, it must be in serious financial trouble.

Putting It All Together

These are the **fundamental steps** to achieving your long-term financial goals.

1. Sock away at least 10% of your take-home paycheck. If you company offers matching funds fro a 401(K), take it and max it out.

2. Define your dividend investment goal in dollars and cents.

> Define how much money you want to have in your hand when you reach your goal. Spell it out in dollars and cents. Declare it explicitly: "I want to have $XX in my hand every (Month, Quarter, etc.)."
> Before you start to buy dividend-yielding stocks, accumulate some cash. Apply my "10%" rule. Max out contributions to your company's 401(K).

> **Start small, and grow big!**

3. Find a broker and using his tools, identify stocks that meet your criteria:

> | | |
> |---|---|
> | Dividend Yield | [>= 9% annually] |
> | Dividend Growth | [>= 5% annually] |
> | Payout Ratio | [35%<->75%] |
> | P/E Ratio | [<= 20%] |

4. Determine when to buy your chosen stocks.

> Don't buy stocks too close to their Ex-Dividend dates.

5. Watch your stock purchases to make sure that they are doing what you want them to do.

But in general, **Leave Them Alone**! Let them do their own thing!

Re-invest your dividends.

In general, don't begin to take money out until your investments are generating your goal's monthly amount.

6. Sell stocks that:

Cut their dividends
Cut their dividend growth
Are acquired by another company
Have a P/E ratio that greatly exceeds 20

Read all you can but read the information with a grain of salt. Don't jump at what someone else says is "**A Great Deal!**" because it just might be a Great Deal for him/her as you 're suckered into some dividend trap, or "Pump and Dump" scheme.

You Have a Choice

Imagine walking into a high-end automobile's dealer's showroom. You and the dealer negotiate a fair price for that dream machine you've always wanted. You sign the contract. The dealer sends someone out to wash and prep your New Car. Then you whip out your checkbook, and buy your dream machine on the spot with cash!

All this and more are well within your grasp.

The possibilities are endless.

All you have to do is…….

 Stretch!

A Final Note

Hey everybody, just wanted to say **THANK YOU,** again, for checking out my book.

I need to ask you a favor. If you're so inclined, I'd appreciate your leaving a rating and a review of *How To Pick Winning Stocks!* on Amazon.

Love it, hate it – I enjoy reading your feedback. It helps me meet my goal of helping you, the reader, and it also helps me in perfecting my writing style.

As you may have gleaned, reader reviews are more important than ever. You, the reader, have the power to make or break a book. If you have the time, please leave me a review.

Thank you so much for spending time with me in *How To Pick Winning Stocks!*

In gratitude,

Jason Jenkins

Appendix - A Practical Formula

We've mentioned a number of ways to assess whether an investment makes sense. We've seen how simple process can be used to sort out dogs from jewels.

Another method is to consider Baron de Rothchild's favorite saying: "Take the 10% and **RUN!**"

Here, we consider how to apply that bromide in the real world.

Let us consider that we want to achieve a particular yield on an investment. To achieve our investing goal, we might like to be able to eliminate stocks that may not have the potential of meeting our ambitions.

As you have no doubt noted from my treatise, there are two paths:

a. Straight accumulation and re-investment of dividends.

b. A more risky path is stock price growth.

Let's explore this second alternative.

Stocks tend to either go up or go down. We can use tools like the "Point & Figure" method to determine what a particular stock may do in the future. But is that prediction enough?

That's what I want to show you in this Appendix.

In a perfect world, profit is defined as:

[Profit = Sale Price - Purchase Price]

But Sale Price(S) = Price per share * number of shares sold.

We're going to buy as many as we sell, so:

Purchase Price(P) = Price per share * number of shares bought.

Let's shorten this:

Pr = S-P

But the real world has other constraints and costs:

1. Each trade cost us money. There's a broker's fee for buying and another broker's fee for selling.

2. Taxes are due on profits. If we hold the asset less than a year, we owe Short Term Capital Gains tax. If we hold the asset longer than 1 year, we pay Long Term Capital Gains tax.

So the profit we actually make can be represented by:

Pr = (S-P) - (Buy fee) - (Sell fee) - (tax owed)

Let's re-write this formula in terms of the purchase and selling prices.

Pr = (S-P) - (Buy fee) - (Sell fee) - ((S-P)* tax rate.)

Let's rearrange that formula to see what price we have to sell that stock at to make a certain profit:

S = P+ ((Pr + buy fee + sell fee)/(1-tax rate))

Example:

We've chosen a stock that is selling for $25 a share. We're going to buy 100 shares. That's an investment of $2500. We would like to make at least 10% on our investment and we're going to hold that stock for 1 year and a day.

Our selected tax rate for this example is 15% - Long Term Capital Gains Tax rate. If you consider holding less than a year, the tax rate goes up to Short Term Capital Gains Tax rates, which is the same as ordinary income. Your rate may be different, so using this formula, you'll have to adjust the tax rate to match your particular situation.

The fees for buying or selling are the same = $8 per trade.

Question: how high does that stock have to rise to make us our 10%:
$$S = \$2500 + (((\$2500 * 0.10) + \$8 + \$8)/(1 - 0.15))$$

Solving:

$S = \$2815.30$. Our stock should at least rise to $28.25 a share to net us a 10% profit.

If this stock doesn't have the potential of achieving a per-share price of $28.25, forget it and move on to the next stock.

Investment Notes

Printed in Great Britain
by Amazon